AF269977

No nā kahu o ka ʻāina. E ola mau
Kanaloa Kahoʻolawe!
—K.H.

To all Hawaiians past,
present, and future
—H.O.

ʻŌLELO NOʻEAU / WISE SAYINGS

He aliʻi ka ʻāina; he kauā ke kanaka.	The land is chief; people are its servant.
E kuahui like i ka hana.	Let everybody pitch in and work together.
I ka wā ma mua, ka wā ma hope.	The future is found in the past.

The True Story
of an Island and Her People

KAHO'OLAWE

KAMALANI HURLEY and HARINANI ORME

Millbrook Press
Minneapolis

In the middle of the great Pacific Ocean
is a little island. Her name is Kanaloa
Kahoʻolawe. She rises from fire.

Kahoʻolawe is born.

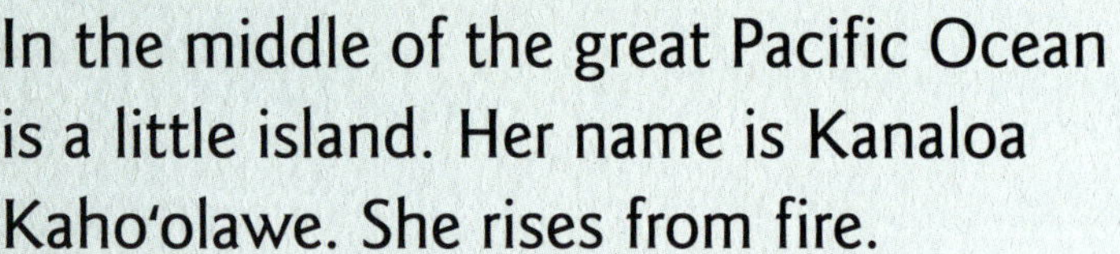

NAMED FOR KANALOA, the Hawaiian god of the sea, the island is a kino lau, or physical form, of Kanaloa. Kaho'olawe is sacred to Kānaka Maoli—the Native Hawaiian people. Nestled next to Maui, the island is the piko, the middle, and the smallest of the main Hawaiian Islands.

The little island teems with life. Naupaka kahakai shrubs cling to the rocky shores. Mōlī and other seabirds soar overhead, searching for their next meal.

Migrating families of humpback whales feed in her warm waters. Spinner dolphins leap and play at Honokanaiʻa, the Bay of Dolphins.

Kahoʻolawe thrives.

FOR CENTURIES the sea surrounding Kahoʻolawe was momona, rich and fertile, with fish, octopus, squid, shellfish, and seaweed. Animals that are currently rare and endangered—the Hawaiian monk seal, ʻopeʻapeʻa (Hawaiian hoary bat), and ʻuaʻu (Hawaiian petrel seabird)—once flourished on Kahoʻolawe.

Polynesian voyagers leave their homes, sailing northward in their canoes over the deep, vast ocean. After a long journey, some of them make their homes on Kahoʻolawe.

They fish and farm and raise their families in the island's abundance.

Kahoʻolawe is happy.

CENTURIES AGO, the ancient Polynesian way finders, guided by the stars and nature's many signs, settled the islands of Oceania. These early voyagers brought canoe plants such as niu (coconut) and kalo (taro) that were key to survival.

Not as lush as the other Hawaiian islands, Kaho'olawe nevertheless offered a good life for the resourceful people who called it home. The scrubland forests provided pili grass that made good thatching for shelters, medicinal plants to keep the people well, and hard woods to make tools, canoes, and houses. Evidence indicates that people lived and worshipped on Kaho'olawe more than one thousand years ago.

One day, a man brings goats to Kahoʻolawe. These animals with big eyes and bigger appetites run wild.
The hungry goats gobble everything in sight. Soon the forests are nearly gone, and rain clouds stop coming.
Kahoʻolawe is thirsty.

WHAT A CURIOUS SIGHT the goats must have been as they trotted off Captain George Vancouver's ship in 1793. Chief Kahekili could not have imagined the destruction this gift would bring. This small herd of feral goats grew to more than fifty thousand by the mid-1800s. Later, cattle ranching was permitted on the island, and the landscape was further damaged. Well-intended efforts to restore the forests failed. Non-native trees such as kiawe (mesquite) greedily drank up ground water, leaving almost nothing for the native trees. Kūpuna, Hawaiian elders, tell of a time when the forests still flourished and the nāulu cloud bridge brought nourishing rains from Maui. When the forests return to Kahoʻolawe and Maui, kūpuna teach us, the rains will also return.

Then, early one Sunday
morning . . .

War!

On the nearby island of O'ahu, bombs fall on Pearl Harbor like rain, burning and sinking ships while sailors sleep.

The next day, the US military seizes Kaho'olawe for practice. It puts targets all over the island and bombs her day and night from the air and from the sea. The military keeps the people away.

WHEN JAPANESE IMPERIAL FORCES bombed the US naval base of Pearl Harbor on the island of O'ahu on December 7, 1941, the United States entered World War II. The very next day, all of Kaho'olawe was seized by the US military. It was now illegal for civilians to set foot on the island. Well after the end of the war, the military continued to occupy the island. For forty years, Kaho'olawe was the most important military training zone in the Pacific.

Kahoʻolawe
is lonely.

Explosions scare off animals and seabirds such as monk seals and manuokū. Missiles that miss their mark break the living coral reefs of this wahi pana, this storied place. The people have had enough!

Stop the bombing! We want Kahoʻolawe back.
But the navy does not stop.

Kahoʻolawe is hurt.

FROM THE 1940S THROUGH THE 1960S, many residents of Hawaiʻi were taught that Kahoʻolawe was a barren rock and that its best use was for military training. For decades people living on Hawaiʻi Island, Molokaʻi, Lānaʻi, and Maui heard regular bombings on nearby Kahoʻolawe that shook windows and rattled nerves. In 1965, a series of tests, code-named Operation Sailor Hat, exploded massive amounts of TNT, cracking the island's underground water table, discharging fresh water that continues to leak into the crater formed by the blasts.

One morning the people board boats and land on Kahoʻolawe.

We're staying! This is our island. We want it back!

But the military forces the people away.

Kahoʻolawe is weary.

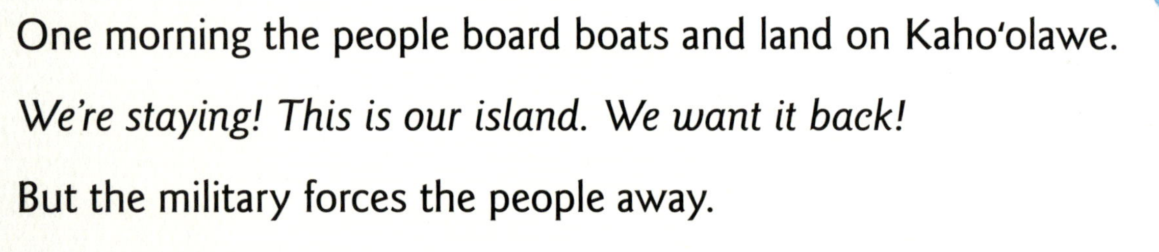

ON JANUARY 4, 1976, nine activists landed on the shores of Kūheia Bay, Kahoʻolawe. Chased all morning by the US Coast Guard, these young people peacefully, although briefly, occupied the island. They hoped this would call the world's attention to the plight of Native Hawaiian people. Two of the activists, Noa Emmett Aluli and Walter Ritte, left the rest of the group to explore the island. The widespread devastation they discovered ignited the movement that changed their lives and the future of Kahoʻolawe.

Soon young Native Hawaiians and their allies organized themselves as the Protect Kahoʻolawe ʻOhana (family). PKO members bravely faced great physical risk and personal sacrifice to lead several nonviolent protests on Kahoʻolawe to end the bombing. Still, the bombing did not stop.

The people are not afraid.
They do not give up,
even when two of them
are lost at sea.

This is our 'āina, our land!
Stop the bombing now!

But the bombing does not stop.

Day after day.

Year after year.

ALOHA ʻĀINA—a deep love of the land—became the guiding principle of the protect Kahoʻolawe movement. In January 1977, two men, Walter Ritte and Richard Sawyer, occupied the island for two months. Hawaiian scholar and leader George Helm and waterman Kimo Mitchell went to bring them off in March 1977, but instead, they disappeared under mysterious circumstances. The loss of these two Hawaiian souls broke hearts and rallied support for the movement. Following many protests and an important court case, Kahoʻolawe was placed on the National Register of Historic Places in 1981. Yet the bombings continued, and Kahoʻolawe is the only place listed on the National Register to have been regularly bombed by the US military.

News of the protests spreads. Soon more and more people feel Kahoʻolawe's pain. They want to help. Their voices grow louder and louder.

Aloha ʻāina! We will protect Kahoʻolawe!

IN 1993 CONGRESS VOTED to end military activities on Kaho'olawe. The following year, control of the island was passed to the state of Hawai'i. It had taken more than fifty years—from 1941 to 1993—for the bombing to stop and for Kaho'olawe to be returned to her people. The military agreed to clean up the island as it had promised to do long ago. Thanks to an agreement between the Protect Kaho'olawe 'Ohana and the US government, Kaho'olawe will become a place where 'ike kupuna (Hawaiian ancestral knowledge) lives.

But when the military moves out,
it leaves a terrible mess behind!

Debris from the bombings litters the land
where plants and grasses used to grow.
Kaho'olawe's reefs are covered in red dirt, and
marine animals and plants struggle to live there.

Kaho'olawe endures.

THE MILITARY'S OCCUPATION had left Kaho'olawe devastated. Much of the island is rocklike hardpan, the result of decades of erosion by the wind and the little rain that falls. Tons of unexploded bombs threaten the island and the surrounding ocean. By 2004, the navy had cleared only about 75 percent of the surface of the island and none of the reefs. The navy left without completing the cleanup it promised to do.

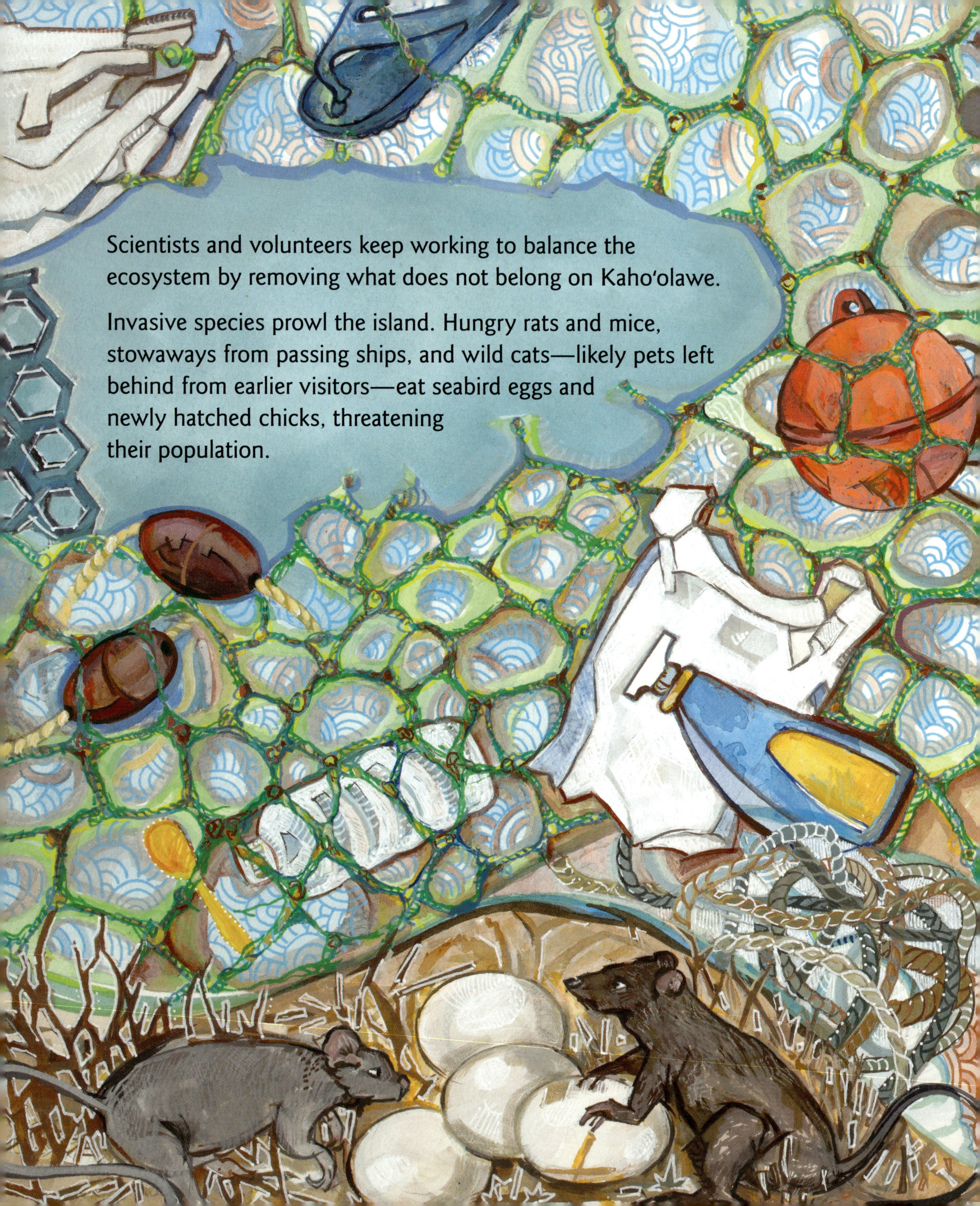

Scientists and volunteers keep working to balance the ecosystem by removing what does not belong on Kahoʻolawe.

Invasive species prowl the island. Hungry rats and mice, stowaways from passing ships, and wild cats—likely pets left behind from earlier visitors—eat seabird eggs and newly hatched chicks, threatening their population.

SEABIRDS PLAY AN IMPORTANT ROLE in a healthy ecosystem. As pollinators and seed spreaders, they help produce new growth and restore the soil. Rats and wild cats are relentless hunters and can quickly destroy whole colonies of seabirds that make their nests on the ground, on cliffs, or in burrows. The fleas these non-native killers carry can transmit diseases that sicken both animals and human beings.

Ocean debris is a major threat to all sea life. Each year, work crews clear away tons of adandoned nets and ropes that can ensnare turtles, sharks, monk seals, and manta rays. The Kahoʻolawe Island Reserve Commission (KIRC) recycles what is salvageable and helicopters the rest to Maui where it's converted into energy instead of being sent to landfills. Unfortunately, by the time plastic debris arrives ashore, it has already done a great deal of damage. Much of it has already been bitten or broken up and swallowed by fish that mistake the brightly colored microplastics for food.

The hard work to restore Kaho'olawe to the
peaceful island she once was continues.

Families and friends, students and
scientists toil together

to renew the natural environment,
to return balance to the ecosystem,
and to pray and heal.

THE ISLAND'S KAHU'ĀINA—her stewards—the grassroots Protect Kaho'olawe 'Ohana and the state government's KIRC, work with many volunteers. They grow native 'a'ali'i and 'ōhai in the uplands to stop erosion and plant 'aki'aki grass to hold down the sand along the shoreline. They build structures to divert rainwater to newly planted seedlings. 'A'ohe hana nui ke alu 'ia—no task is too big when done together.

Kaho'olawe lives.

The people will never give up.

Kaho'olawe, the little island in the great Pacific Ocean, was nearly destroyed. But her spirit will never be broken.

The people love Kaho'olawe. And Kaho'olawe loves the people.

Kahoʻolawe aloha ʻāina.

KAHOʻOLAWE IS UNIQUELY HAWAIIAN. Environmentalists draw on Indigenous science methods, comparing new observations to historic ones. Archaelogists record the ruins of ancient homes and temples, now totaling 3,800 historic sites. Builders construct kauhale gathering spaces as well as platforms for hula and celestial navigation training. Cultural practitioners lead spiritual ceremonies, such as the annual Makahiki that celebrates Lonoikamakahiki and the bounty of the ancestors.

Adding Western technologies, such as desalinating seawater into fresh drinking water, helps Kahoʻolawe to become the piko of Hawaiian cultural and environmental learning.

With so many caring people working together, Kahoʻolawe truly lives.

AUTHOR'S NOTE

Kahoʻolawe is the story of the aloha—the love—the Native Hawaiian people have for the ʻāina and for one another. This is the true story of a remarkable group of young Native Hawaiian activists who risked everything to fight environmental and social injustice and dared to take back the ʻāina from the greatest military power on Earth. Like many Native Hawaiians of my generation, I had heard that Kahoʻolawe was a barren rock, and for a long time I believed those stories. The Hawaiian Renaissance of the 1970s opened our eyes to the history, language, and cultural traditions that had been taken from us. When my youngest daughter went on a science huakaʻi—a trip—to Kahoʻolawe, she returned filled with a renewed pride in being Hawaiian that continues to inspire our ʻohana. This book is dedicated to the many kahuʻāina—stewards—both past and present of Kanaloa Kahoʻolawe.

ILLUSTRATOR'S NOTE

It was such an honor to be asked to illustrate a children's book about the island of Kahoʻolawe. After reading the manuscript several times, I started to visualize the different options for each scene. Being a Native Hawaiian artist, I felt it was both my kuleana (responsibility) and an opportunity to contribute by adding the visuals to this important story about the history and cultural restoration of the island.

Shortly before completing these illustrations, I met with Davianna McGregor, a member of the Protect Kahoʻolawe ʻOhana who helped steward the lands of Kanaloa Kahoʻolawe. While we were talking story, I told Davianna it was my dream to go to the island, and on the spot she invited me to join a group of volunteers to go to Kahoʻolawe. I immediately said yes! By seeing and touching the ʻāina, I was able to connect even more deeply with the story told in this book. Kahoʻolawe has a unique beauty and mana (spiritual energy) that cannot be described. My experience further enabled me to become a part of the healing of the island.

Mahalo (thank you) to Kamalani Hurley for telling the story of Kahoʻolawe island for young people. Mahalo also to Lerner Publishing Group, PKO, KIRC, Davianna McGregor, Craig Neff, the six women and men Kua facilitators of PKO accesses to Kahoʻolawe, boat access captains and crew, photographers Ian Lind and Franco Salmoiraghi, and friends for being so gracious in sharing their experience and knowledge of Kahoʻolawe's history with me. Mahalo to those who continue to mālama (care for) this island. Finally, mahalo to the brave men and women who fought relentlessly to stop the bombing of Kahoʻolawe and to take back this sacred island.

Harinani Orme took this photo from Hakioawa Bay, Kahoʻolawe.

TIMELINE

circa 400 Polynesian voyagers settle the pae ʻāina (the Hawaiian archipelago). Earliest evidence of settlers on Kahoʻolawe dates to 1027.

1793 British captain George Vancouver gifts goats to Maui chief Kahekili. By 1941 the uncontrolled goat population reaches fifty thousand.

1848 The Māhele becomes law, introducing the concept of private land ownership. Kahoʻolawe is owned by the government of the Hawaiian Kingdom.

1858 The Hawaiian government permits ranching activities on Kahoʻolawe. Overgrazing by goats, cattle, and sheep devastates the island's ecosystem.

1893 On January 17, businessmen backed by the United States stage a coup d'etat and illegally overthrow the Indigenous government. Control over Hawaiian government lands is under the American-led provisional government.

1941 On December 8, the US Navy seizes Kahoʻolawe for military training purposes. This is one day after the imperial Japanese military bombed Pearl Harbor at nearby Oʻahu island.

1953 US president Dwight Eisenhower officially gives control of the island to the US Navy. Kahoʻolawe becomes known as the Target Island.

1959 On August 21, Hawaiʻi becomes the fiftieth state.

1965 To simulate an atomic bomb attack, the navy conducts Operation Sailor Hat on Kahoʻolawe. In one of three tests, the navy detonates 500 tons (454 t) of TNT, resulting in Sailor Hat Crater.

1969 The navy accidently drops a half-ton (0.5 t) unexploded bomb on a Maui cow pasture. US representative Patsy Mink unsuccessfully demands a stop to the bombing of Kahoʻolawe.

1976 On January 4, the first of several peaceful protest landings on Kahoʻolawe begins. A newly created grassroots organization, Protect Kahoʻolawe ʻOhana (PKO), files a lawsuit in federal court to stop the bombing and accuses the US Navy of environmental and cultural offenses.

1977 In March two PKO members, George Helm and Kimo Mitchell, are inexplicably lost at sea off Kahoʻolawe. That year the Department of Defense begins its survey of ancient archaeological sites, identifying over 540 sites in three years.

1981 Kahoʻolawe enters the US National Register of Historic Places. However, military training, including bombing runs, does not stop.

1982 PKO holds Kahoʻolawe's first Makahiki, traditional Hawaiian celebrations, in over one hundred years.

1990 President George H. W. Bush temporarily orders a halt to the bombing. The Kahoʻolawe Conveyance Commission is appointed by the US Congress to recommend the future use of the island.

During Operation Sailor Hat in 1965, 500 tons (454 t) of TNT are detonated.

1992 PKO holds a healing ceremony on Kaho'olawe. In less than a year, the US Congress officially ends all bombing and budgets $400 million to clear the island.

1994 On May 7, in a ceremony on Maui, Kaho'olawe is officially returned to the state with the promise that one day a "sovereign Hawaiian entity" will take it over, forever protecting the island from commercial development.

2004 The US Navy completes its work to clear Kaho'olawe of ordnance although only about 75 percent of the island's surface and virtually none of the surrounding ocean have actually been cleared.

2013 After over forty years of continuous Native grassroots and governmental efforts, members from PKO, KIRC, the Office of Hawaiian Affairs (OHA), and others establish the Kanaloa Working Group to lead a plan for cultural restoration and conservation work on Kaho'olawe.

2024–present Work on cultural and conservational restoration continues.

Kūpuna Eddie Ka'anana, restoration coordinator Penny Levin, and hardworking volunteers plant kou honuala (native sugarcane) to help fight erosion.

GLOSSARY

aloha 'āina: deep love of the land

huaka'i: journey

'ike kupuna: ancestral knowledge

Kaho'olawe: a small island located 6 miles (10 km) southwest of Maui, also known as Kanaloa Kaho'olawe and Kohe Mālamalama (figuratively, "a sacred place that nourishes")

Kānaka Maoli: the Native Hawaiian people

Kanaloa: one of the four major akua (gods)

kino lau: physical form of a deity (literally, "many forms")

kahu'āina: stewards of land

kuleana: responsibility

kūpuna: elders

Māhele: an 1848 law that changed traditional land management into the Western concept of private ownership of property

Makahiki: traditional religious festivities celebrating Lono, the god of agriculture and rain, and the harvest, land, and family

momona: rich, fertile, fat

nāulu: rain cloud formation

'ohana: family

pae 'āina: archipelago, a group of islands

piko: center (literally, "navel")

wahi pana: sacred space

HOW YOU CAN HELP

In Hawai'i, both KIRC and the PKO welcome volunteers. Workdays are challenging and can be difficult. Unlike the other islands, Kaho'olawe is an arid, harsh landscape. Because safety is an important concern, both groups require orientation. You don't need to be in Hawai'i to help the land: you can also help conservation efforts right in your own neighborhood. Many organizations offer activities such as cleanups and planting days where you can help fight climate change and make the world a more livable place. Ready to get started? Ask your teacher or school club advisers for help with ideas. Be a part of the environmental 'ohana where you live!

ADDITIONAL CULTURAL AND ENVIRONMENTAL RESOURCES

Visit the author's website, www.kamalanihurley.com, for enrichment activities, additional notes, pronunciation guides, and links to teacher resources, articles, photos, music, videos, and more.

SELECTED REFERENCES

Kaho'olawe Island Reserve Commission
http://www.kahoolawe.hawaii.gov/home.php

Kanaloa 2026 Working Group. "I Ola Kanaloa! A Plan for Kanaloa Kaho'olawe Through 2026." Protect Kaho'olawe 'Ohana. 2014. http://www.kahoolawe .hawaii.gov/plans/I%20OLA%20KANALOA.pdf.

Protect Kaho'olawe 'Ohana
http://www.protectkahoolaweohana.org/

Source for the 'Ōlelo No'eau: Pukui, Mary Kawena, *'Ōlelo No'eau: Hawaiian Proverbs and Political Sayings*, Honolulu: Bishop Museum Press, 1983, no. 531, 323, 6.

Mahalo nui loa to Dr. Davianna Pōmaika'i McGregor, 'Anela Evans, and the Protect Kaho'olawe 'Ohana, and to Michael Naho'opi'i of the Kaho'olawe Island Reserve Commission for their expertise and support.

Millbrook Press™
An imprint of Lerner Publishing Group, Inc.
241 First Avenue North
Minneapolis, MN 55401 USA

For reading levels and more information, look up this title at www.lernerbooks.com.

Photos: Harinani Orme, p. 30; U.S. Navy Photo/Naval History and Heritage Command, p. 31; Ilina Loomis/The Maui News via AP, p. 32.

Designed by Danielle Carnito.
Main body text set in ITC Goudy Sans Std.
Typeface provided by Adobe Systems.
The illustrations in this book were created with Liquitex Arcylic Gouache.

Library of Congress Cataloging-in-Publication Data

Names: Hurley, Kamalani, 1955– author. | Orme, Harinani, illustrator
Title: Kaho'olawe : the true story of an island and her people / Kamalani Hurley ; illustrated by Harinani Orme.
Description: Minneapolis : Millbrook Press, 2025. | Audience: Ages 7–11 | Audience: Grades 2–3 | Summary: "Discover the story of the smallest Hawaiian island, a place sacred to Native Hawaiians, from its formation long ago to its present-day restoration as a protected site. A remarkable narrative accompanied by stunning illustrations" —Provided by publisher.
Identifiers: LCCN 2024022793 (print) | LCCN 2024022794 (ebook) | ISBN 9798765605011 (library binding) | ISBN 9798765659113 (epub)
Subjects: LCSH: Kahoolawe (Hawaii)—History—Juvenile literature. | Kahoolawe (Hawaii)—History, Military—Juvenile literature. | Kahoolawe (Hawaii)—Environmental conditions—Juvenile literature.
Classification: LCC DU628.K255 H875 2025 (print) | LCC DU628.K255 (ebook) | DDC 996.9/22—dc23/eng/ 20240705

LC record available at https://lccn.loc.gov/2024022793
LC ebook record available at https://lccn.loc.gov/2024022794

Manufactured in the United States of America
1-1010932-51421-7/29/2024